Level
2

The Nature Kid's Guide to
WALRUSES

DAVID ANDERSON

LP Media Inc. Publishing
Text copyright © 2026 by LP Media Inc.
All rights reserved.

No part of this book may be reproduced or transmitted in any form or by any means, electronic or mechanical, including photocopying, recording, or by an information storage and retrieval system — except by a reviewer who may quote brief passages in a review to be printed in a magazine or newspaper — without permission in writing from the publisher.

For information address LP Media Inc. Publishing,
30012 Variolite St NW, Princeton MN 55371
www.lpmedia.org

Publication Data

Walruses
The Nature Kid's Guide to Walruses — First edition.

Summary: "Learn all about Walruses, the Nature Kid Way"
— Provided by publisher.

ISBN: 979-8-89818-146-8

[1. Walruses – Non-Fiction] I. Title.

Title: The Nature Kid's Guide to Walruses

CONTENTS

ICY WATERS

DID YOU KNOW?
A walrus can hold its breath under water for up to 30 minutes while hunting for food!

Splash! A huge walrus dives into icy Arctic water.

Walruses live in some of the coldest places on Earth. They swim in the Arctic Ocean, where the water stays near freezing all year long. Big chunks of ice float on the water all around them.

These animals love the ice. They climb onto ice floes to rest and warm up in the sun. A **floe** is a flat piece of ice that floats on the sea.

The water is very cold, but walruses do not mind. Their bodies are built for the chill. Home sweet home is a world of ice and snow.

ARCTIC ATLAS

Roar! A walrus calls out from a rocky beach on the frozen Arctic coast.

Walruses live near the top of the world. You can find them close to the North Pole. They roam the coasts of Alaska, Canada, and Russia.

There are two types of walruses. Pacific walruses live near Alaska and Russia. Atlantic walruses live near Canada and Greenland. Both types stay in cold, icy seas.

Walruses follow the ice as it moves with the seasons. In winter, they travel south. In summer, they move back north. The ice is like a moving highway that takes them where they need to go.

HEAVYWEIGHTS

Thud! A giant walrus flops its heavy body onto a block of ice.

Walruses are really, really big. A grown male can weigh as much as a small car. That is about 3,000 pounds!

Females are a bit smaller, weighing about 1,800 pounds. But that is still very heavy. Even a small walrus is as heavy as a full grown horse!

A walrus can be 11 feet long, that's longer than a basketball hoop is tall! All that size helps them stay warm in freezing water.

Among seals and sea lions, only elephant seals are bigger than walruses!

TERRIFIC TUSKS

10

Clack! Two walruses bang their long, pointy tusks together.

Both male and female walruses have tusks. Tusks are really long teeth that grow from the upper jaw. They can grow up to three feet long!

Walruses use their tusks in many ways. They dig them into ice to pull themselves out of the water — scientists call this the tooth walk, which is actually how the walrus got its scientific name! They also use their tusks to smash breathing holes up through the ice from below.

Tusks show other walruses who is boss. The walrus with the biggest tusks often gets the best resting spot on the ice. Size matters in the walrus world!

WHISKER WONDERS

Walrus whiskers are so sensitive they can feel a clam buried under six inches of mud!

Swish! A walrus sweeps its whiskers across the dark ocean floor.

Walruses have about 700 thick whiskers on their snout. These whiskers can sense tiny things. They work like fingers that feel and touch.

The ocean floor is very dark. It is hard to see down there. So walruses use their whiskers to feel for food in the mud. Each whisker is as thick as a piece of spaghetti.

Every whisker can move on its own. When a whisker bumps a clam or snail, the walrus knows just where to dig. Those whiskers are like built-in treasure finders!

TOUGH TANKS

Walrus skin turns pink when warm and pale white in cold water!

Slam! A large walrus scans the horizon for polar bears.

A walrus has very thick skin. In some spots, it is almost two inches thick! That tough skin is hard for teeth and claws to get through.

Under the skin is a thick layer of fat called **blubber**. This blubber can be six inches deep. It keeps the walrus warm in freezing water and pads the body like armor.

When danger comes, walruses use their tusks to fight back. A jab from a sharp tusk can scare off even a hungry polar bear. Most predators learn to leave adult walruses alone.

CLAM CRAZY

Munch! A hungry walrus finds a bed of clams on the cold sea floor.

Clams are a walrus's favorite food. They also eat snails, worms, and other small sea creatures. A hungry walrus may eat over 4,000 clams in just one day!

Walruses like to eat in shallow water. The sea bottom is full of tasty treats. Lots of small animals hide in the sand and mud, waiting to be found.

Sometimes walruses eat crabs and shrimp too. They are not very picky. If it is small and lives in the sea, a walrus will try it!

SEAFLOOR SLURP

Walruses do not use their tusks to dig up clams like scientists once thought!

Whoosh! A walrus squirts water to blast away sand and find its food.

A walrus does not chew its food. It uses its lips and tongue to suck the meat right out of a shell. Slurp! It works just like a vacuum cleaner.

First, the walrus digs in the mud with its snout. It pushes its nose along the sea bottom to find buried clams. Then it squirts water from its mouth to wash the mud away.

Once the clam is free, the walrus sucks out the soft parts and drops the shell. The sea floor is covered with empty shells after a walrus finishes eating!

DANGER LURKS

Growl! A walrus spots a polar bear creeping across the ice.

Polar bears and orcas are the main predators of walruses. A polar bear may try to catch a young walrus on the ice. But grown walruses are tough to attack.

Orcas hunt walruses in the water. A group of orcas may team up to chase one walrus. They are fast and strong swimmers who work together.

Adult walruses are so big that most enemies leave them alone. The biggest danger is for young calves. They are small and cannot fight back yet, so their mothers guard them closely.

STAY SAFE

FUN
FACT!
Walruses can swim up to 22 miles per hour—3 times faster than an Olympic swimmer!

Crash! A herd of walruses rushes into the sea to escape danger.

When a walrus spots danger, it heads for the water. Walruses are much faster in the sea than on land. Splashing into the waves is their best escape plan.

On land, walruses stay close in big groups. Being in a crowd helps keep everyone safe. It is harder to grab one walrus when hundreds are packed together.

In the water, walruses can dive deep to get away. They swim fast enough to escape most threats. The sea is their safe place, and they know it well.

WADDLE
SWIM

DID YOU
KNOW?
A walrus has flippers that bend
backward to help it walk on ice
and rocks!

Plop! A walrus slides off a big ice floe and into the cold sea.

On land, walruses are slow and clumsy. They waddle on their **flippers**. Each step looks a bit silly, like a heavy sack being pushed along.

In the water, everything changes. Walruses become graceful swimmers! They push with their back flippers and steer with the front ones. It is like watching a different animal.

Walruses can swim for a very long time. They paddle along for hours without stopping. They can also float on their back to take a rest at sea.

LAZY DAYS

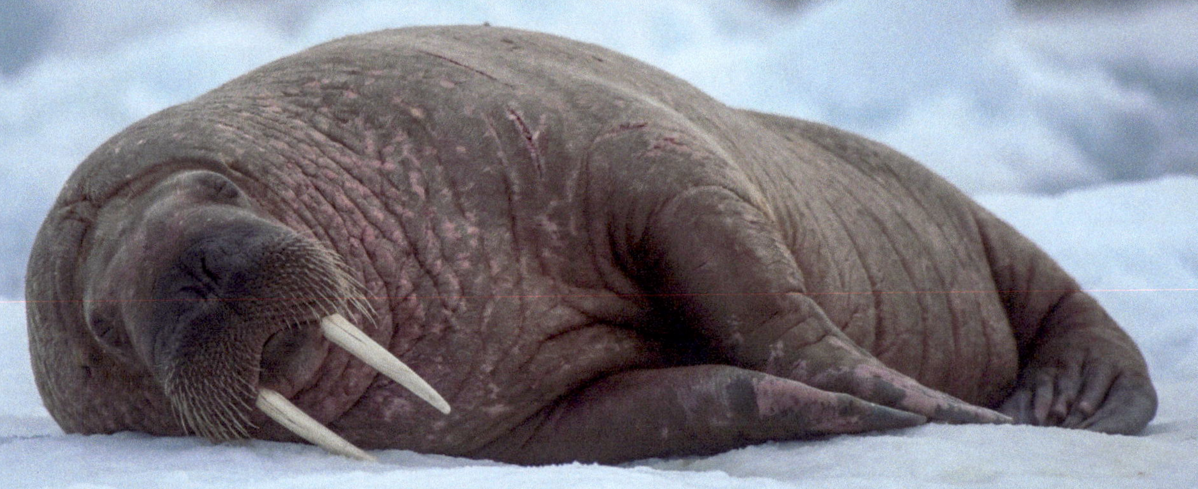

A walrus can stay awake and swim for more than three days in a row without rest!

Snore! A big walrus naps on the ice with dozens of friends nearby.

Walruses spend a lot of time resting. After a big meal, they climb out onto the ice or a rocky shore. Then they take long naps in the sun.

Some walruses rest while others keep watch. They take turns sleeping and eating. This helps the group stay safe from danger at all times.

Walruses also spend time in the water each day. They swim, dive, and hunt for food. Then they come back to rest and start all over again. It is a simple life of eating and sleeping!

HUGE HERDS

A big group of walruses resting on a beach is called a haul-out!

Bark! Hundreds of walruses crowd together on a rocky Arctic shore.

Walruses are very social animals. They love being around other walruses. You can find them in groups of hundreds or even thousands!

A group of walruses is called a herd. Males and females often stay in different herds. The males go one way, and the females and calves stick together.

When they rest, walruses pile on top of each other. They do not mind being squished! The warmth of so many big bodies keeps everyone cozy in the cold Arctic air.

BELLOWING BULLS

Bull walruses sometimes battle each other with their tusks, leaving scars on their thick skin!

Bong! A male walrus makes a deep, loud bell sound under the water.

Male walruses are called bulls. In winter, bulls try to impress the females. They make loud sounds under the water, like bells and whistles.

Bulls puff up special pouches in their throat to make booming calls. They sing and splash to show off. The louder and longer the song, the better!

Females listen and pick the best singer. Mating happens in the water during the cold winter months. It is quite a show in the icy Arctic sea!

CUTE CALVES

DID YOU KNOW?
Walrus milk has about ten times more fat than regular cow milk!

Squeak! A tiny walrus calf crawls on the ice and gives a soft cry.

A baby walrus is called a calf. Calves are born in the spring on the ice. They weigh about 100 pounds at birth. That is big for a baby!

Newborn calves have soft, gray fur. They can swim right away, but they are not as fast or strong as the adults yet. They stay close to mom.

Calves drink their mother's rich milk. It helps them grow fast. In just a few months, they get much bigger and stronger. Soon they will be ready to dive for their own food!

MAMA KNOWS

DID YOU KNOW?
Walrus mothers sometimes adopt and care for calves that lost their own mom!

Grunt! A tired baby walrus rides back to shore on her mother's back.

Mother walruses take great care of their calves. A mom stays with her baby for about two years. She teaches it how to find food and stay safe.

Calves ride on their mother's back in the water. When they get tired, they hold on tight. Mom does all the swimming for both of them!

If a polar bear gets close, the mother will fight. She puts her body between the bear and her calf. Walrus moms are some of the bravest mothers in the animal kingdom.

MELTING ICE

DID YOU KNOW?
Up to 35,000 walruses have been seen packed onto one single beach when ice runs out!

Crack! A walrus watches its ice floe break apart in the warm sun.

The biggest threat to walruses is **climate change**. As the Earth gets warmer, Arctic ice is melting. Walruses need that ice to rest, have babies, and find food.

With less ice, walruses crowd onto beaches instead. Too many walruses in one spot can be dangerous. Small calves can get stepped on in the crowd.

Oil spills and pollution also hurt walruses. Dirty water can make them sick. The Arctic is changing fast, and walruses need our help to survive.

HELPING HANDS

FUN FACT!

Click! Scientists observe a walrus to track where it swims and rests.

People around the world are working to help walruses. Scientists study them to learn what they need. They track walruses to see where they travel and rest.

Some countries have laws that protect walruses. In the United States, it is against the law to hunt them. These rules help keep walrus numbers safe.

You can help too! Saving energy at home helps slow climate change. When we take care of the Earth, we take care of walruses and all the animals that share our planet.

GLOSSARY

Arctic

The very cold area near the North Pole

blubber

A thick layer of fat under a walrus's skin

floe

A large, flat sheet of ice floating on the ocean surface

climate change

A slow warming of Earth that melts ice and changes weather

flippers

Flat body parts that help walruses swim

www.ingramcontent.com/pod-product-compliance
Lightning Source LLC
Chambersburg PA
CBHW041621110726
48005CB00002B/466